Tender vulner... narrative of jou... into their own... power of God's .... to each of us. Their story will change stories—including yours.
          -Ronne Rock, advocacy journalist, speaker, and author

Deedra and Megan invite you into their stories so you can invite others into yours. With sensitive transparency, they reflect openly on the bondage, brokenness, and pain that shaped their lives. Their stories will move you. You may even see yourself in their experiences. As they share the tenderness and power of Jesus, who met them at the place of their greatest need, you will get a glimpse into the Savior's great love for His daughters and His desire to see them live free. Every one of us needs His love and His ministry of freedom. We can access it when we examine our stories and bring them into the light. Many avoid doing this but Deedra and Megan, through their own powerful testimonies, share what life is like when we stop hiding and open up the dark places so they can't hold us hostage anymore. *Walking Dauntlessly* is a powerful book that will give you permission to look bravely at your past so you can unlock a future filled with freedom, grace, loving relationships, and a confidence that God has a purpose for your story."
          -Aurora Gregory, Communications Strategist and Co-Author of the Amazon bestseller, "Get Picked"

Walking Dauntlessly tells the story of how God used the broken to create something beautiful. I have been privileged to witness firsthand the healing and transformation that has happened through the ministry that is Dauntless Grace. I was there when God began to form this ministry and it has been an honor to watch this story unfold.
          -Tracy McGee, founder of All Your Heart Ministries

If the Bible communicates any storyline consistently, the Scriptures tell us that God has the power to change everyone's story and give those who call upon him a new beginning and a new ending. No one needs to be held captive in a tale of sorrow, pain, or rejection. Dauntless Grace is a ministry dedicated to helping people discover their redemptive narrative. Deedra's and Megan's testimonies will inspire you to begin the wonder-filled experience of re-writing your story.

- Dr. Patti Amsden, pastor and author

When you see your life as a story, something changes inside. When you determine to walk dauntlessly into the thick of your story, everything changes. This book will help you do both.

- Mike Loomis, writer and coach

Me, too. We want to know we are not alone in our doubts, our struggles, and our fears. *Walking Dauntlessly* will have you nodding in agreement, whispering, "Yes. Me, too." You will be inspired and encouraged to live a life of dauntless faith.

-Michelle Discavage, author, speaker, and Certified Life Purpose Coach

Walking Dauntlessly

The Search for a Meaningful Story

Megan Hall & Deedra Mager

Walking Dauntlessly

Copyright © 2016 Megan Hall & Deedra Mager.

All rights reserved.

ISBN 978-1537669595

Truth Productions

PO Box 47

Troy, IL 62294

www.dauntlessgraceministries.org

Walking Dauntlessly:
The Search for a Meaningful Story

Table of Contents

Prologue: The Backstory of this Book — 7

Exposition: Setting the Stage of Our Stories — 13

Inciting Moment: Writing Our Own Stories — 17

Rising Action: De-Creating the Broken Story — 21

Climactic Moment: Letting Jesus Rewrite Our Stories — 29

Falling Action: Where Our Stories Collide — 35

Resolution: Living His Story for Our Lives — 55

Epilogue: Connecting You to a Meaningful Story — 61

The Backstory of this Book
Prologue

Megan

While sitting on an airplane on the way home from Colorado, I leaned over to Deedra Mager, my closest friend and ministry partner. "Let's outline our book," I said.

We had spent a week in the Rocky Mountains as part of an intensive workshop for ministries, writers, and entrepreneurs ready to take their dreams to the next level. The workshop, produced by Launch Out, gave us the tools to really define our mission and propel Dauntless Grace Ministries into the future.

During the workshop, I felt the need to tell our stories, both of us as individuals and us as friends, in a book that explained the fundamental ideas behind Dauntless Grace. I scribbled on a piece of paper, "Our first book is going to be called *Walking Dauntlessly*."

Instead of making resolutions at the New Year, both Deedra and I had embraced the idea of choosing one word to define our year. For 2016, God impressed upon me the word *walk*. While I know there was an obvious physical connotation (start doing laps at the track) and even a spiritual connotation (spend more time in the Word and in prayer), embracing the word went even beyond that.

Everything about 2016 was up in the air. I had a job teaching at a Christian school until May, when the doors closed for the final time after a 34-year legacy. I had no idea what was on the horizon. Would Dauntless Grace be enough to supplement my income? Should I continue the master's degree I began the year before? Where would my oldest daughter attend school? Should I send queries to agents to publish a novel that I had been writing?

I felt like Abraham. God told me to walk, but He didn't tell me where I was going.

Deedra chose the word *dauntless* for 2016. Like me, her future held no clarity. She was working at the same Christian school and had many of the same questions I had. Should she find another paying job, or would God grow our ministry? Where should her kids go to school now? Even though she had no answers, she knew that God was gracing her with a new boldness for the year, and she would choose to live dauntlessly.

Walking Dauntlessly not only encompasses both of the stories of our own healing, but it shows how God took a year of unknowns and unclear questions and moved us in the direction of His choosing.

And so we began outlining our book on an airplane. Several miles in the air, God met us in a holy moment and gave us the framework for the story He wanted us to tell.

Because both of us have taught English classes, we decided to embrace our inner nerds and tell our stories using the plot chart in literature: exposition, inciting moment, rising action, climactic moment, falling action, and resolution.

Our stories are not extraordinary testimonies. However, whether we were shaped by big events or small, we are all defined by the circumstances in which we have lived. This book is our process of throwing away our old stories and walking dauntlessly into new ones.

More than anything, it is our prayer that you will find your own story in these pages. We pray that you'll see how God is moving you into your own meaningful story.

Charting a Story

Exposition: The story's context

Inciting Moment: The story's conflict

Rising Action: The story's unfolding

Climactic moment: The story's revelation

Falling action: The story's new beginning

Resolution: The story's meaning

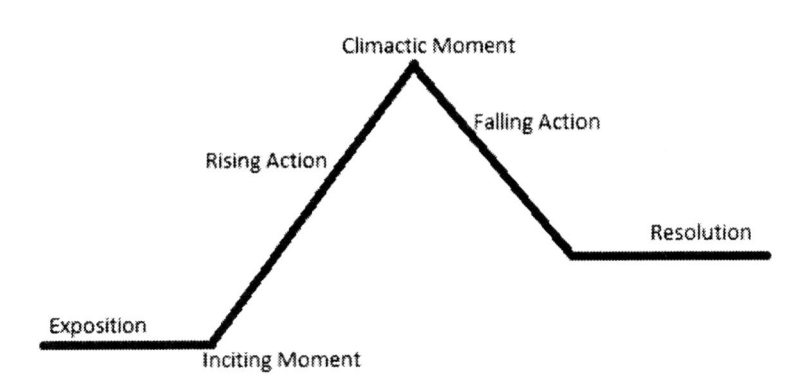

Setting the Stage of Our Stories
(Exposition: The story's context)

Deedra

I grew up with a quieter disposition in the middle of a large family with even larger personalities. I had trouble with the concept of being heard and being seen. How is one heard over the din of four siblings and two parents, all of whom are natural-born leaders and extroverts? How is one seen in the midst of so many others' talents and accomplishments? I had issues with my skin and features that I did not feel fit the definition of "pretty." From terrible fever blisters, rashes, and sunburns to early onset acne, I learned by fifth grade how to hide myself with makeup and hairstyles. Large pores, large nose, broad face, frizzy hair—these were the bane of my pre-teen existence! Naturally, I did not want others to look at me.

Then struggles that were more internally focused emerged as I began to venture into the junior high phase of relationships. I had friends who labeled me as their best friend. They wanted an exclusive relationship with me. I felt as though they used up my time and energy, not allowing me to foster other relationships, and then they moved on to another "best" friend once someone else more fun came along. I was a pastor's kid in a small school, so I was an easy target for girls who wanted to climb the social ladder. I was popular but usually because people knew me before I knew them. I didn't really want anyone to see me in this way, either.

I kept busy, very busy, learning to talk fast to get the necessary words into a conversation, learning to zoom in and out of a room behind the facade of a task, and keeping plates spinning so others would look at the things I would do instead of simply seeing me. By the time I was a very young adult, I was in charge of several church departments while attending college and getting married. I didn't have down time. I didn't want it. Busyness was my mode of operation. The activities replaced the relationships. The hiding replaced the longing for true friendship. The accomplishments replaced simply being. But not for long.

It's not how we are wired. We are made for relationship. God created in each of us a longing to know and be known, to love and be loved. In fact, I knew very well the theology of unconditional love. I had been a Christian in a Christian home, school, and church in which my doctrine of salvation was well rehearsed. Jesus loved me and died for my sins! Yes! In my head, I understood—but the distance from head knowledge to heart transformation is a long one.

I had some lonely seasons because I was surrounded by things to do and people I love, but I did not know how to make a connection at the level I truly desired. I was doing the work of the ministry and raising babies and being a friend and a wife. I was loving God and serving Him, but the self-protective walls around my heart were too solidly entrenched for authentic connections.

I felt like the Samaritan woman in John 4 who encountered Jesus. Busy with her day-to-day activities, she was not expecting to meet the One who would transform her life. She came to the well to draw water. This was a simple task, something she no doubt did daily. She may have been thinking about what she was making for dinner or rehashing a recent argument in her own thoughts. She may have been rehearsing a difficult conversation she needed to have once she returned home. I am sure she was busy building her story in her own head, because we all do it all of the time. On her way to draw water from the well, she was writing some kind of script for herself to follow. Undoubtedly, she had determined her role long before that day and she was living out the narrative that she had unwittingly written.

Writing Our Own Stories
(Inciting moment: The story's conflict)

Deedra

In 2001, I was 25 years old, had been married for almost four years, and had a one-year-old son. My church was hosting a Bible college intensive one weekend, and I was listening to the speaker, intent on her message. Her teaching focused on Christian counseling and the pathway to freedom. We were in the last day of the three-day seminar, and she began to tell a story of two young girls to whom she had ministered. Her story resonated with me. Then she got to a particular part of their story that involved the codependency of their relationship.

A wave washed over me: memories, shame, panic.

I quickly ran from the classroom, escaping the stares of others. Tears blurred my vision as I ran down the hallway to seek isolation. I found an empty office and crouched in the corner, sobbing. My heart felt like a scab had been pulled away from a very deep wound. I couldn't breathe; I couldn't stop the tears. I had uncovered a painful realization. A childhood relationship with an older friend that had become twistedly codependent came to my memory. The abuse and the loss of sexual innocence that went along with that were also uncovered.

I can't say that I had repressed the memory in a clinical sense, but I certainly had not thought about it in a long time and had suppressed the issue in an attempt to hide the shame. When I was very young, I had an older friend who had claimed me as a best friend and I had desperately wanted to please her. This did not prove to be a healthy friendship. Even when I grew up and realized that it had been wrong, I never told anyone.

Throughout my tween and teen years, I realized that my pattern with friendships was that I would give all my time and energy to someone so as not to disappoint them, and then I would be discarded when they no longer had any use for me. I was a people-pleaser, and I got sucked into needy relationships because I didn't know healthy boundaries. I remember often begging my mom to tell me no, that I couldn't go to a friend's house, because I didn't know how to say it and wanted her to be the bad guy. I spent many days depressed at the thought of all the obligations I had instead of enjoying my friends.

At that seminar, a huge piece of the puzzle popped into place. I had known I was a people-pleaser; I had known

I felt like something was wrong with me, that I was blemished in some way. But I had never had the grace to look at the root cause, which is that I was absolutely tarnished by abuse and was terrified that someone would discover it.

I imagine I felt like the Samaritan woman, afraid that someone would see all my sin, all my imperfections. However, right there at the well, in the middle of her everyday activities, she encountered this man in such contrast from any man she had ever known. He offered her a drink that was different from the water she had always consumed. If she felt like me, I could believe that she was longing for something new that could truly satisfy. She was probably intrigued with the idea of quenching that thirst.

Perhaps fear was present, a certain amount of trepidation at the unknown. Nevertheless, she had to be ready for change and was likely desperate to know the way to happiness. Her own attempts to find that path had left her feeling empty and lost. At least in my story I knew that I had come to the awareness that the script I was writing was not going to give me the ending I desired. My awareness of my pain and emptiness drove me to find a new story.

De-Creating the Broken Story
(Rising action: The story's unfolding)

Deedra

After I became aware of the abuse in my past, I had to process my healing. It began the moment I had to speak the words out loud to someone. At that same conference for Christian counseling, my mother noticed that I had left the room and had not returned. She came looking for me, concerned that I was sick. When she found me in the fetal position, hiding and sobbing, I couldn't find the words to tell her. Shame was a palpable weight. My eyelids were so heavy that I couldn't even keep them open to look at her. Once she held me and I began to find my breath, I uttered a few incoherent words. It wasn't a full story, but it was enough. She understood and she cried with me. It was a start.

The instructor offered some counseling time to me after the seminar was finished. She and my mother helped me to process as much as I could at that point. They led me through prayers of forgiveness that began the hard work of redemption in my life.

After that, I began to speak about it more to my husband, my mother, my sister, and a few trusted friends.

The conversations were hard and awkward, but I had to have a safe place where there was permission to release the toxic, repressed memories. I also had to begin to learn how this abuse informed my current thinking about relationships.

The shame of abuse had caused me to be ultra-self-protective of my personal space, time, and energy. So, I began to make myself step out of my comfort zone to give to others who were hurting. I started learning to set boundaries in those places so that I didn't give in to them out of the emptiness of my fear but instead out of the abundance of who God was in me. However, it was scary. It was hard. I felt unprotected and raw. The usual layer that had been between others and me had to get peeled back, and that was an uncomfortable process.

I had learned a counseling model in my church that is in large part contributed to the work of Dr. Larry Crabb. I grew up understanding that we all have an image based on how we see ourselves, but we don't really know what that is because it does not register at the cognizant level. My image was formed by many factors, from temperament to birth order, from circumstances to victimization. When I was very young, I began interpreting my world through the lens of all of the things that had made up my exposition. The experiences I lived began to paint a picture of who I thought I was.

Because I, like all of humanity, was born into sin and my parents were great but not perfect, and because I had experienced my own kind of victimization, my image was marred. I did not believe that I was truly the child of the King. This broken image brought me shame. So I did what we all do and I tried to hide my true, flawed self from others. In order to hide, though, I had to fabricate a story about myself that was a different truth from the one I really believed.

I believed that I was flawed and marred by abuse. I didn't quite have a handle on the exact image I viewed of myself. I just knew that I was desperately hiding my shame in order to keep people from seeing the flawed me. I adopted the belief that I needed to be perfect, fully mature, so that no one would know I was imperfect. I thought that if I could stay busy and keep others' eyes off me and on what I was accomplishing, no one would stop to see my inadequacy.

Allowing others behind my mask of perfection meant letting them see the real me. That was too risky. Instead, I kept a wall of separation between others and me, a hand up saying, "Keep your distance." I could continue to look good if you saw me from just the right angle and just far enough away. Besides, why would I get close enough to let someone use me or abuse me again?

As I was recognizing the brokenness in my old story, the healing process began. I began to see the truth about my self-protection. It was sinful. I was protecting my own heart instead of trusting God to be my fortress and my deliverance. I had constructed a wall to keep my distance from others and in so doing had constructed a wall to keep God out, too. Don't get me wrong—I wanted to serve Him. I wanted to glorify Him with my life. My desire was to do the work of the Kingdom. But to sit in His presence and commune with Him terrified me! And to serve others by just being present with them without a purpose to hide behind was also frightening!

During that same time, I was having babies. I had our first son right before the counseling seminar in which I experienced my awareness moment. After that I had a miscarriage and then two more babies by the time our oldest was four. I had three littles at home, the two girls only sixteen months apart. Technically, I was a stay-at-home mom, but I still worked in our church office part time and also ran the youth group, dance ministry, and any productions that our church did for holidays and conferences. This was my volunteer work that I did during nap times and late at night. I found my life in those places of serving.

It became increasingly more difficult to wear all of those hats as I was dealing with fairly severe morning sickness, sleepless nights, nursing, potty-training, and toddler tantrums! There were many days that I was running on sleep deprivation and felt like a rubber band stretched as thin as it could go. When it finally snapped, I was a mess!

I remember the day the last fray popped. I'm sure my husband does, too! It was 2003. I was planning a mission trip for our worship team and I was going to take our five-month-old with me as I was still nursing her. I had one too many irons in the fire and she was screaming, my three-year-old was throwing a fit, the dishes were piled up in the sink, and laundry was waiting. I had to finish the conference schedule for our trip's itinerary and I couldn't get that simple task finished. I also knew that I still had all of my personal clinic teachings to prepare and choreography that I hadn't even started. My goal of looking perfect was getting majorly blocked! How in the world had I gotten all these plates spinning? Every single one of them was about to crash.

In a complete panic, I couldn't catch my breath and I started screaming! Not at anyone in particular. In fact, I just locked myself in my room and screamed. Here I was, a normal, sane, Christian woman just trying to serve in her church and raise her babies, and I was completely losing it! My husband came in a little later and said, "We need to get you some help!"

Of course, that only upset me more. I started sobbing. I couldn't let him tell anyone. I didn't even want him to call my mom. She raised five children and did all kinds of ministry work. I don't remember her losing her marbles because of it. Why couldn't I make it work? Why didn't I live by the fruit of the Spirit that I had just taught my youth group teens the week before? Something was wrong with me, and I didn't know how to get back to normal.

Despite the chaos leading up to departure, I boarded the plane for that mission trip. I still had not reached out for help, and I was anxious. However, I knew somehow that God was going to meet me. I was desperate for change and knew that time away to hear His voice might be my only chance for finding my sanity.

Here's the thing—that trip was amazing! God had set me up to be completely exposed so that He could begin to minister to the parts of my heart that I had kept hidden from Him. As I finally let down and admitted to my mom that I had lost it and I was afraid I wasn't going to get it back, she showed me it was normal. I had an unattainable goal of looking perfect blocked in a way that even my skilled maneuvering couldn't work around. Blocked goals equal anger, and this anger was worse than it had been in the past because the stakes were higher. Now I was dealing with not being able to be a perfect mother. I had no control over when my kids would need me, and I would not be able to accomplish the other tasks that I had committed to doing.

It was a gradual start, but I began to relinquish control. It was daunting to stand on the precipice of an uncharted journey, an unknown tale. Slowly, I began to hand the pen back to the Author of my story. Very slowly, I began to say no to things that I had always done because I so desperately needed them to keep me busy. Even more slowly, I began to give myself some grace as a mother who was not perfect. And eventually I started recognizing the triggers before they became panic-inducing.

During that season, I felt that for every step I took forward in my victory over old mindsets and wounds, I took two steps back in bondage to my sinful self. But the truth is that God was moving me forward toward Him through it all. I began to trust that the healing He offered was a more secure place to be than the fort of protection that I had constructed in my brokenness.

How did the Samaritan woman at the well feel when Jesus called her out? He saw right through her lie and said, "You are right in saying you have no husband; for you have had five husbands, and the one you now have is not your husband." She must have felt shocked, even exposed. How did He know these things? I felt that I had come to this point, as well, in my life. The sin that confronted me demanded that I look at it. There was no more hiding, no more shifting focus off me to deflect attention, no more lying about my true self. I had a choice to make: would I continue to craft a story of my own making that was characterized by self-deceit, or would I recognize that the plot I was charting was a mess? I had to acknowledge my brokenness.

Letting Jesus Rewrite Our Stories
(Climactic moment: The story's revelation)

Deedra

After baby number three came and turned one, I was excited to face a year of doing what was really in my heart to do. I got to participate in three mission trips in 2005. One was a worship conference to Panama. During our time in Panama, our team had a time of worship as part of an evening devotion in one of the hotel rooms. The Lord turned our time together upside down that night! There was such a beautiful presence in the room. All of us sat there for three hours in mostly silence, with some people weeping, some quiet, some lying down. I have been in some crazy charismatic worship settings in my lifetime, but that moment on the floor in a hotel room in Panama was the most life-changing for me. I knew that Jesus had come in the room.

I didn't see Him with my natural eyes, but I felt His presence more strongly than I ever had before and ever have since. I realized that I was a woman with a soul-bleeding issue. I had diagnosed it, but I saw no cure. I didn't know where to find the solution. I had read books on the subject of finding victory after abuse. I knew the Lord. I had opened up to some very mature Christians who were walking alongside me. But there wasn't a day that went by that I didn't wonder when the bleeding would stop. There wasn't a moment of silence where I didn't feel the emptiness of my heart and wonder if there was more to life than this false narrative.

But in that moment? Well, in that moment, I knew I could reach out and touch Jesus. His very essence could make me whole. There was just a sure knowing in me that He was there to heal me, that He was present and close. I am sure that I heard Him calling me to draw near to Him. It was frightening. It was unprecedented. I felt naked. But I did not feel shame.

No, in that moment with Him, I reached for Him, and all of the power of the Creator was at my fingertips, all of the life of the I Am was within my reach. And it was just one touch that forever stopped the bleed in my soul. The issue of death that had been sucking my life was eradicated in that split second.

He showed me my image as I had never seen it. I saw myself as a dirty sponge. I had value as long as I worked for Him, as long as others could use me. But I was so afraid that someone would take a moment to stop and look at that gross dirty sponge. What if they did? Would they see the disgusting mess I was? The thought made me shudder. In an instant I saw that picture, and I realized that I had arranged my life to keep the focus off me. It began to make sense that my perfectionism wasn't about being perfect; it was about being busy. I had known that staying busy was my mode of operation, but I hadn't before seen why. It was about not allowing others the time to inspect the mess.

At the very same moment, God gave me a new image. I was clean. I was whole. I had a heart that was not damaged. I had transformed into something white and pure; I was not defiled. And it was translucent. His glory was literally shining out of my heart. The walls were down, and I was a vessel that was ready to let His light shine out of me. He had done a work of transformation. I didn't have to let love leak out of the broken cracks as I hurriedly tried to reserve enough time and energy for myself. I had abundance because I was filled with Him.

I got up from the floor, wiped my eyes, and worshipped! I was free! I don't even know how to describe the incredible weight that had been lifted from me on that cold, hard tile floor! But I do know that I have never been the same.

I began to share my story without shame. I began to more quickly recognize old patterns of behavior that would creep back into my lifestyle. It took several more years to be able to walk free from the sin of perfectionism (and, let's be honest, I'm still not perfect at being imperfect)! Oh, but I know grace. And I know the freedom that comes when my protective layers fall away and I trust in the One that promises me life and life everlasting! I am able to face the daunting task of now living a new story—His story. His story is one of redemption.

Whenever anyone encounters Jesus, they are changed. The Samaritan woman at the well was a beautiful example of this. She perceived Jesus was a prophet, but He wanted her to understand He was the Messiah. Her eyes were opened. He was the Promised One, the Savior. That revelation held hope and stirred her heart to seek forgiveness. The result was an epiphany of true worship.

I have experienced this in my own life. When I came to the realization that Jesus is the only One who could heal me, I had to relinquish control. That act is similar to bowing down in submission. It is true humility to declare His lordship in my life. Worship is the act of bowing low as He is lifted high. Authentic worship is in spirit and in truth (John

4:24), and I experienced that kind of worship when I encountered Jesus as the very source of my life. In that moment of transformative healing, I put down my pen and handed it back to the true Author of my story.

Where Our Stories Collide
(Falling action: The story's new beginning)

Megan

    I first met Deedra at a back-to-school teacher meeting in the fall of 2010 when I was 27 years old. While I had probably seen her around before, I hadn't officially met her until she began working as the secretary of the Christian school where I was entering my second year of teaching. I remember asking others about her before I met her; I enjoyed the camaraderie of the office and was hoping it would continue after she began managing it.

    Throughout that first year of working together, we saw each other very little. I was only working part time that year because of my two-year-old at home, and leaving each day at 11:00 wasn't conducive to forming relationships in the workplace. At the staff Christmas party that year, I filled a plate with appetizers and sat down on a bench at the long dining room table in our principal's home. Deedra carried her plate over to me and asked if she could join me on the bench. We had a fairly large staff that year, and I felt honored that she chose to sit by me. From what I had seen of her personality, she was friendly and outgoing, and people seemed to be drawn to her. I was no exception.

Of course, it was a pattern that I already recognized; I tended to find a woman, usually a little older than I was, who exuded qualities that I admired, and then I latched on tightly. This pattern had brought me nothing but broken friendships and heartache over the course of my life. Mentors moved far away. A teacher switched to a different school. A boss took advantage of my hero worship and manipulated me, eventually betraying me. Friends grew weary of my constant need for affirmation and affection and pulled away.

I knew I wasn't able to form healthy, God-centered relationships with women, but I didn't know how to break the cycle.

Exposition: The story's context
Megan

I am the youngest of three. My older brothers were 10 and 7 when I was born, so I was very much the baby of the family. My whole life, I wanted a sister to look up to. When my brothers brought girls around the house, I hung on their every word and tried to be like them.

Because my brothers were good friends and because I never had the sister I craved, I often felt alone, isolated, and rejected. Though I had friends at school and church, I felt like I was on the fringes, like I was unnecessary. I never felt as cool as they were; I always felt immature and a step behind. It seemed that everything I had learned about becoming both a teenager and an adult came from the books I read or the shows I watched. Even as I grew older, the desire for an older female role model never faded.

That unfulfilled desire came crashing over me in October of 2011. I was at a revival service at Deedra's church. The worship was more charismatic than I was used to, but the presence of God was very real. As I witnessed people experiencing the touch of the Father through exuberant worship, something broke within me. Deedra and my friend Heather began praying for me. Heather said that she had this picture of me in a jail cell with bars all around. I was looking out and seeing everything, but I wasn't experiencing it with others. Sometimes the door would swing open, but I was content to grasp the bars and watch. In that moment, I first realized that I was living in bondage, even though I had been a Christian in a Christian home my whole life.

Inciting Moment: The story's conflict
Megan

For about a year, I learned more about the power of the Lord. I began to pray and minister over others, but I was

My fear was so strong that night that I was almost panicking. I texted Deedra: "Do you have any idea of the expectation I had for this weekend? Thinking that, for once in my life, someone wouldn't let me down? But all I did was get let down again, build up walls that weren't here last week, and possibly drive a wedge in my relationship with you."

She responded, "You can look at it that way, or you can see that God is giving you an opportunity to find Him in your brokenness."

I read her response and began crying, and then texted, "Why does this always have to be hard? And painful? And to what end? For what purpose?"

She said, "Because the egg shell is cracking, and it will never get put back together again. He's tearing down the walls that separate you from Him, and deconstruction is messy. Stop using other people to deflect intimacy with Him."

I knew things had to change in both my relationship with God and in my relationship with Deedra. The next Monday at school, I asked Deedra if she could recommend some discipleship tools that could help me begin the process of healing. By the grace of God alone, she agreed to meet with me during my planning period.

Deedra

I had major warning lights going off that night at the service. I could feel her need for me to make things better, to provide an emotional cushion for the pain she was feeling as her deepest longings were being exposed. I had spent the whole service feeling guilty because I knew she was upset. Truly, I was feeling trapped and frightened that I had found myself in a place of having to meet a need. I hadn't signed up for this, but I didn't know how to say no.

I thought we were work friends, acquaintances, sisters in the Lord, but I didn't have time to invest in going deep. I was trying to figure out how to balance going back to work full time, ministering in several areas of the church, and raising four children, the youngest of whom still had major sleep issues that left us awake for two to three hours most nights. I felt that I had close relationships with quite a few women already, and I didn't have time for more. Plus, I was mentoring some teens and trying to find the balance between making time for them and protecting time with my young children. I wasn't looking for a best friend or even a peer who needed spiritual mentoring. I wasn't looking for quality time outings that took me away from other responsibilities and relationships I already had. There was a selfish motivation to protect myself, my time, my energy.

I knew Megan wanted to mature in her walk with the Lord. She was aware that there were soul issues that needed to be healed. But when there was an opportunity for her to kneel at the altar and touch God, she sulked in the back of the church. I am sure I did not handle this well. I am quite certain my words were not completely born out of a righteous anger when I told her to find God or leave. In fact, I'm sure that God was using me in spite of my selfishness. His spirit was moving in her heart despite my lack of sensitivity.

Rising Action: The story's unfolding
Megan

The process of healing is so messy. As God began chipping away at the walls I had erected around my heart, I found myself raw and open but not yet healed. Things were stripping away—old patterns, behaviors, and protections—but I hadn't let God fill in those missing places with His love and forgiveness. I remember feeling such pain, like I had lost a layer of skin. I was exposed, and I had nothing covering me from myself or from others around me. I was vacillating between anger and depression. I was angry because I wanted to be completely healed; but since it hadn't happened yet, my goal was blocked. The depression was because I couldn't get clarity on my own issues; the confusion and lack of answers triggered deep melancholy within me.

Over the course of many months, God began revealing the innermost parts of me in a slow trickle. In one particular meeting with Deedra, I began to realize painful words I always used to describe myself: annoying, frustrating, unworthy, selfish, clingy, suffocating, unwanted, unchosen, inferior, ignored, and immature.

Another night, after conducting parent/teacher conferences, I had once again been left out of an invitation to go out with some colleagues. By "once again," I don't mean that they always left me out. Far from it, actually. But it felt like yet another example of how in my life, I feel like I'm always on the fringe of the fun. If I'm there, it's fine, but if I'm not, no one really misses me. This has always been a struggle for me, even with my own family. While I have always had several groups of friends, I've not felt as if I am a vital part of any of them. That night, as I was driving home, I felt the word *unwanted* scream through my brain, and I began to cry. I seemed to be getting closer to the truth about who I thought I was.

Weeks later, as I was praying, God revealed an event from my childhood from when I was about 4 or 5 years old. Though the event wasn't about me specifically, I remember feeling pushed aside during a traumatic event that happened in our neighborhood. I felt like I needed to be as quiet and small as possible so as not to be a burden on everyone who was truly dealing with the trauma. An older girl in the neighborhood had to babysit me because my parents were busy helping with the scary events of the night.

The connections should have seemed so obvious to me. But at the time, when God was slowly peeling back the layers of healing, remembering this event still felt like one more piece of the puzzle that I was frustratingly trying to jam into place. I couldn't figure out how everything connected or what the image was that I had of myself.

While all of these revelations were occurring, I was falling back into behaviors that hadn't crept up on me in years. My dependence on Deedra for help and affirmation was palpable. My thoughts and words were like the mindset of an immature teenager or a child. It felt like I was regressing, not moving forward. So many times, I tried to quit the process. I didn't want to uncover any more pain. Thankfully, neither the Lord nor Deedra had given up on me. She was committed to holding my feet to the fire.

Deedra

I felt God nudging me to take my walls down. Graciously, He was giving me a heart of compassion for someone else to taste the freedom that I was beginning to express. I really believe that I began to understand for the first time that someone else's brokenness had nothing to do with me. I wasn't responsible for fixing it. I didn't need to fill longings for love or acceptance. Only God could do that. All my life I had known this in my head but not in my heart.

Of course, God is the only one who can satisfy the deepest longings of our souls! For so many years, I had entered relationships to fill voids and to keep myself busy so that no one inspected me. I needed to re-learn how to set healthy boundaries that were not based in self-protection. God was maturing me to see that I had been healed so that I could be a vessel that His pure love could flow through to connect others to Him. It wasn't about me at all. I didn't have to fear being used by someone for their own gain and being left empty. He was enough. He was enough time, energy, love, and healing for any need. I didn't have to be. I just had to let Him be.

Because I began to understand God's healing and unmerited grace, I knew that I could connect Megan to the same One who had healed me. I had been the recipient of healing even though that process had taken years and years to journey. I knew that she, too, could taste that same freedom. When she wanted to give up, I encouraged her to continue in her pursuit of truly knowing Him. Some days, I walked beside her as we faced the daunting task of embracing the journey of healing together. Some days, I walked ahead of her as a role model of freedom in an area where she was struggling. Now that I had experienced freedom, I found that I didn't need to give anything to her except to continue to lead her to the beautiful Savior who was offering everything she had need of.

    Just like the Samaritan woman, I was ready to tell another about the One who had forgiven me. It was my joy to offer the hope of Living Water that would truly satisfy the soul thirst of my friend. I knew that she had already known Jesus Christ as her Savior, but there was so much more! There was a deeper revelation of who He was that she needed to experience. My response to my own healing was to tell another of the source of my wholeness and the revelation of living in true worship.

Climactic moment: The story's revelation
Megan

God showed me a picture of a toddler.

I can't remember now if it was a dream or an image I received while praying, but it happened one night, probably two years after I had begun the process of healing. Toddlers are whiny, needy, clingy, and often burdensome (I know this because I've raised two of them).

Though at times they're cute and fun to be around, toddlers can generally be a nuisance. Their immaturity means they can't make healthy decisions for themselves; they will often touch or taste what they shouldn't. Their ignorance implies that other people are constantly cleaning up their messes. And their neediness means that wiser people have to guide them and shower them with affection.

I saw myself in that picture.

I believed at my core that I was a burdensome, bothersome nuisance. I was immature, ignorant, and needy.

My heart broke while I was lying in bed. Through flowing tears, I recognized the truth that without Jesus, I would remain all those things those things. I had a lot of safety guards in place to appear less of a nuisance to those around me. I relied on my book-smarts to mask the ignorance and inadequacy that I felt. I embraced my teenage mindset to prove that immaturity is funny and acceptable. And I needed affirmation and affection so much that I pulled too hard on those around me, eventually pushing them away and validating my own deficiency.

In none of those defense mechanisms had I allowed God to work. It was time for my repentance. Though I had no control over my birth order, the event that occurred when I was 4, or the personality I had been given, I could certainly control my sinful choices as a born-again believer. Every time I tried to extract life from my defense mechanisms, I was telling God that I knew how to fix me better than He knew how.

I knew in that moment that I couldn't live any longer in a broken story. As much as I had tried to protect my heart, I had failed. My heart was shattered, both from my own doing and from how others had responded to me. I couldn't try to write my own story any longer.

I confessed all my defenses to the Lord, and asked Him to heal me from the bottom up. I thanked Him that His blood had covered my sins and that His Spirit had granted me wisdom, maturity, and confidence through no work of my own. I no longer wanted to live how I had been living. Even though it might be painful, I wanted to hand the pen back to the Author of my story. I knew His grace would be enough to cover the fear I felt about living a new story.

Deedra

As we worked together and went to church together, our friendship was based on proximity and shared interest. This is more than likely always the beginning of a friendship. However, because of the walls that I erected to protect myself and because of Megan's need for an older friend to mentor her, our relationship had taken more of a mentor/mentee pattern in its early phase. I had walked further in life and natural maturity than she had just because I was older, and I had processed more of my healing journey than she had at that time. I was content with this as long as she needed me to show her the way, but I was still cautious to use the label *friend*. That word held a lot of baggage for me.

However, as transparency and honesty began to break down our walls, I was more open to what God was doing. He was forging a friendship—one that would test my old ways and require me to choose a different path. Because we don't get to see how a story ends as we walk it out, it takes dauntless faith to trust that God is leading. It also takes faith to believe that He will protect even when my own self-protection layers are set aside.

As I began to walk a new story in this friendship, I allowed myself to become vulnerable, to share my time and energy I had previously guarded. We met outside of work to have coffee, to take the kids to the park, to ride together to events. I found that the camaraderie I felt was becoming reciprocal. I was enjoying our times together because I wasn't on the defensive. She wasn't draining me. I didn't need to waste energy protecting myself.

At the point of writing this book together, things are different. Now I can be the real me and Megan can be free to be herself. We can choose to have hard conversations to figure out what triggered our responses or emotions. We don't relate perfectly. Some days we walk in old patterns. But we can point that out to one another. This encouragement helps each of us to identify the old patterns and choose to give the pen back to God to continue authoring our story.

One moment of awareness, one place of repentance does not create a new story. It is the daily habit of walking dauntlessly in community.

Falling action: The story's new beginning
Megan

Repenting of my own sins of protection, and forgiving anyone who made me feel inadequate or unwanted, was a huge step forward for me. However, my story didn't end there. I had to choose repentance and a new story over and over again.

On one occasion, Deedra and I were driving to the airport to travel together. I am not a big fan of flying, but more than being afraid of crashing, I panic about airport security. This didn't make any sense to Deedra. While I know that it's a simple process—take off your shoes, put your bag in the bin, and walk through the metal detector—my heart would race and my palms would sweat every time I stood in line. I wasn't afraid of being pulled to the side or that I would get "caught" with contraband; in fact, there was no reason for the fear. That day, Deedra looked at me and said, "God is going to reveal a new level of healing for you in this area." Then she went on to say that the panic I felt in security lines was similar to the panic I felt when I took my toddler out in public. While she was right about the similar feeling, I didn't see any connection between the two events.

A few days later, in our hotel room, I was struggling to fall asleep. My mind kept going back to what she had said about figuring out why I panic in airports. And then I realized—I was afraid to hold up the line and make someone else wait behind me. Similarly, I didn't like taking my two-year-old out to dinner because I was afraid she'll make too much noise or a mess.

"I figured out why I panic in those situations," I said the next day. "I don't want to bother anyone."

"That's it," Deedra agreed. And she reminded me of my image of being a nuisance. Then she explained that I panicked because in both of those situations, I couldn't control the circumstances. I couldn't control if I held up others in the security line or if my child was too loud in public. The lack of control and the fear of being a nuisance combined to create a panic within me that had, some days, immobilized me. But with this new awareness, I no longer had to live in bondage to that fear. God was peeling back a new layer of my defenses, and I was ready to submit to Him.

All the pieces of my healing were—and are—out there; I simply wait for God to help me connect all the pieces of the redemptive story He is writing.

Deedra

Here's the beautiful thing about really knowing someone: we can see past the initial layers to the heart of what is happening. The words which God is faithful to give in a specific moment of time are clarifying, laser-focused, and Spirit-driven. They shine light on an unilluminated part of our hearts to bring us further healing. Counseling is important. It brings awareness of pain and creates paths for healing. But accountability of that truth in community is where the rubber meets the road.

Truth has to be walked out. Truth has to be applied to real life. Then truth leads to new pathways.

If I hadn't known Megan the way that I did, I would have rolled my eyes at her fear. I would have dismissed it as something I could not relate to. If I hadn't understood her parenting fears from the point of relationship where I could see it from her side, I wouldn't have had much to impart because it didn't make sense to me. However, I had walked a path with her and had seen what God was doing in some of the rawest moments of that process. And I knew that this was the next layer of understanding for her. It was a divine appointment for a key that God was giving her to unlock old mindsets that had her bound in fear.

Also, it is important to note here that as we began to discuss the image she was seeing of herself and how that had informed so many of her past decisions and current fears, we also saw some patterns where those fears had affected our relationship. I was able to repent for places where I had added to her shame instead of helping her overcome. She found language for the paradox that she had felt but hadn't been able to earlier communicate. It was a moment of healing both for her personally and for our relationship.

Living His Story for Our Lives
(Resolution: The story's meaning)

Megan

It's been five years since I first became aware that I was living in bondage, and it's been two since I handed the pen back to Jesus, the Author and Perfecter of my faith. Each day I have to choose freedom. And some days I'm better at that than others.

In March of 2015, a few years into my healing, I received a rejection letter from a publishing company telling me that I had not made it into an author's launch team. That rejection hit the deepest levels of pain in me, and I sobbed. Like, sitting on the edge of my bed, hair in my face, clutching my blanket sobbed over a rejection email that was sent to 4500 women (at random) because 5000 people applied for 500 spots.

Maybe that pain was about more than not getting an advanced copy of a book. Or maybe it revealed that I had some more healing to face.

In a Twitterstorm of activity following that email, I saw a tweet that referred to those of us who didn't make it, and a group was formed on Facebook for all of us who still wanted to support the author's book launch.

I reluctantly joined this group, still upset but ready to see what this new group would be about. I knew it would take several weeks for the chaos of introductions and remembering people's names to settle down. Instead of trying to wade through the confusion of a brand-new group, I decided to get real with the ladies in the group. I began asking questions of the women that required them to be transparent and honest with themselves.

Eventually, those vulnerable threads began clouding up the newsfeed, so several of us moved to a separate group where we could be more open and real with each other. It was amazing to see the raw, vulnerable stories of some of these women. The very nature of social media is to put up a veneer, yet we chose to strip it off and get real.

And God began moving.

Because of the willingness of these women to be authentic and bare, we began to see healing. Women shed long-time insecurities and gained new confidence. The women began fiercely praying for each other's marriages and families. Lifelong friendships formed.

But, even there, I stayed in the background of my own group.

You see, I was still dealing with the pain of rejection—the pain of feeling like I wasn't wanted by the author or her publishers in the "real" group. And I realized that I was also finally coming to grips with some rejection issues I had pushed aside in my real life. Even on the other side of my climactic moment, of the awareness that I needed to repent and hand back the pen, I was still running into pain.

I was down. I don't know another way to put it. I wasn't depressed, but I couldn't lift my head. It didn't feel like a familiar battle. I told Deedra that I felt like I was standing on the edge of something, and I could either jump toward what God had for me or I would surely fall into something I wouldn't be able to get out of. She looked me in the eyes and told me that I was trying to live again out of my brokenness. I was attempting to go backwards and live out the old story I had hidden behind for so long. She said it was time that I acknowledged my healing. She said that God had a new way of living for me where I needed to be ready to minister healing to others. And that was a conversation that tipped the scales.

I jumped into the new story, into the unknown where God was giving me authority I never asked for or wanted.

I knew God had something special planned for the women in this Facebook group I had formed. I didn't believe it was an accident, and I knew He wanted us to take all the good, hard things we had been experiencing in the virtual group and move them into our real lives. He wanted us to share our stories.

God told me to start a ministry based on this concept. So I did.

Dauntless Grace Ministries has been alive since May of 2015. For almost two years, it has existed as a blog, Facebook page, and online community. It wasn't until the workshop in Colorado that Deedra and I realized the clarity of vision to take God's healing into churches. You see, community happens in churches. It happens in the workplace. It happens when people commit to "doing life together," like Deedra and I committed to do several years ago.

Healing doesn't occur in isolation. Healing is found in the context of those communities. It happens when we reach our arms up towards God and out towards each other.

Life together is messy. Walking out the healing process in relationship is painful. Even since writing this book, Deedra and I have found ways to push each other's buttons and cause pain, anger, and confusion. When humans are in relationship, we hurt each other. The good news is that, with the clarity God has graced us with and the humility we both embrace, we now can quickly become aware of the issue and apologize before we sever the ties on a God-ordained friendship.

Deedra

Sometimes we think we've given someone permission to speak into our life, but there is a difference between having a friendship and making a choice to walk out a process of healing with someone. Some of the greatest pain I've experienced as a more mature believer is when I thought that I was in a friendship where we both desired truth and healing, only to discover that the pain of the process made the other person jump out of the relationship.

I have laid down my self-protective layers in an attempt to bare the parts of my soul that needed transparency the most. But when a person walks away from the process, it is difficult to not take it personally. It is painful to lose the depth of relationship. I have learned, though, that it is not my fault, and that God has a path for each of us. If I am not the one that God is using to walk another through to complete freedom, He has someone else for them. But I am not giving up on the desire for deep relationship and community. Despite past failures in this area, I daringly reached out to Megan to forge a new story, one of living transparently in authentic relationship.

When I drink from the well of living water, I want to share it with others. Merely telling them about Jesus is not enough. I want to take them by the hand and lead them to the well. Extending my hand to them and journeying with them to the place of encounter is the delight of my heart! It is the greatest story!

Connecting You to a Meaningful Story
Epilogue

Many Christians have had a change in their spirit (their eternal being) because they are alive in Christ and they have heard messages that have informed their minds with information. But so often, they still allow their souls (emotions, mind, will) to be informed by their flesh (their bodily senses that have experienced joy and pain).

Like both of us, many women ask, "Is this all there is? What if there's more? Am I even worthy of a better story?" They don't feel satisfied with the story they're living. Desperate to find meaning, they try to rewrite it themselves.

Dauntless Grace Ministries is connecting women to a meaningful story. We begin by bringing a two-day conference to a local church. This conference, through teaching and worship, fosters awareness of the broken stories women are living. Awareness alone does not create transformation. Transformation is the result of living transparently in community and choosing to walk dauntlessly into the new story that God is writing.

In the first eighteen months of the ministry, women like Tori and Cassandra experienced transformation through the community of Dauntless Grace.

Tori

Most people would look at my life and be hard-pressed to find something that I need to be healed from. I would, too. I've lived a vanilla cupcake life, honestly. My parents are still married to each other and are believers. I became a believer at a very young age, and I've never felt any need to stray from the Lord. I graduated from a Christian high school, then attended and graduated from a Christian university. I met my husband at college and we got married about six weeks after we graduated. He also comes from a family where the parents are still married to each other and have walked with the Lord his whole life, so he has walked with the Lord his whole life, too. I have no tragedies to point to as turning points. No extended periods of soul-tearing grief or sorrow.

But the truth is, we live in a fallen world. The Enemy whispers to me just like he does to everyone else, and I'm a weak human who listens sometimes. I've been fairly good at reading the Bible and praying on a consistent basis for my whole life, but even in the midst of that I began to believe that I wasn't worthy of a better life because mine was good, that I am not a person who is worthy of having lifelong friends, only seasonal ones who will move away from me to things that are better for them. Those moments of listening have done deep, under the surface damage. This damage has made me sensitive to situations that should be harmless, but whenever they would occur I'd scramble to hide myself at home, pouring my woes out Psalm style in my poor, abused journal.

It's easy to keep living how we're living, believing the things we've believed about ourselves. Most of the time we don't know better. Sometimes it's just comfortable, even in the midst of the pain. We know what the pain feels like. We don't know what our life will look like without it. But try to imagine what life will look like if you live according to the Truth, rather than the lie. If you can't imagine it, I understand. But know that it is possible.

Over a year ago, I joined a Facebook group, a group dedicated to being honest and speaking Truth to each other and what later became the basis for Dauntless Grace Ministries. And as I look back, that is where my healing began.

Through discussions and book recommendations and prayer, my life is different than it was a year ago. These ladies have gently pushed me away from that ledge I was clinging to, the ledge built on lies I believed about myself. To my surprise, there was no giant drop or anything. I just had to step away, turn around and walk toward Truth. When I hear the lies calling, the Holy Spirit speaks through these ladies to remind me of the Truth, and I can focus again. Normal, innocuous daily instances that used to cause me pain don't anymore, because I am able to recognize them for what they are. Usually the things that happen are not about me or my shortcomings at all.

Several months after our group formed, I participated in a discussion, and several people contacted me privately to celebrate the healing they saw in me. It was very strange. I didn't even know I had been healed; I wondered what I had been like before. But enough of them said it, so I began to look deeper. Sure enough, I realized that those lies just didn't get my goat anymore. I can dismiss them almost without a second thought. I am in awe that the Holy Spirit still works like that in me, polishing away rough edges until even I don't remember what they were like before. He not only healed my heart, He healed my memory from feeling shame or regret over the way things were.

It's been the prayer of my heart for my whole life: "Make me like You." Most of the time I worry about that, trying to figure out what I can do to make myself like Him. But by filling my life with Truth-speaking friends, I didn't even have to do anything. He did His work, gently, quietly. And I feel peace.

Cassandra

One year ago there was a girl living in the shadow of shame. She was angry and felt really small. She punished herself for betraying her husband after a night of drinking while he was deployed. It was a single night that would define her for the next six years. She would isolate herself and berate herself. She avoided God because she couldn't handle any more conviction. She was not nice to her children. She was controlling and insecure and suspicious of her husband. She was so lonely and alone.

But then she came across an online group. They claimed to be real and want to love and encourage each other and point each other to God. She decided to test the waters. She told her ugliest ugly secret. She was prepared to leave when the truth was known. But that's not how it happened.

Her truth was known. She was still loved. She was accepted. She was led back to the truth of who she was IN GOD, and not defined by that "Thing" she had done or the person that shame had created. Little by little, this online community helped her to heal. The light shone into her soul. She began to hope again. Eventually, she forgave herself and accepted God's forgiveness. That girl transformed from a shadow into a light.

That girl was me. Me! This girl! She remembered that as a child of the one true King, she was saved, redeemed, beloved, precious, and important in God's work.

DAUNTLESS GRACE

Transformation through Story

Bring a Dauntless Grace conference to your local church.

Many Christian women are not actively participating in a local ministry. They're often dissatisfied with activities or afraid they won't measure up to others who seem to have it all together.

The *Transformation through Story* conference is not your typical women's event.

It is about connecting women to a meaningful story.

This two-day experience is designed to facilitate a breakthrough moment. Worship, teaching, stories, and honest conversation will foster authentic community.

For churches ready to launch a new ministry, we offer post-conference curriculum for small groups and provide online support for leaders.

To book a Dauntless Grace conference at your church, contact us at conferences@dauntlessgrace.org
or visit our website at www.dauntlessgrace.org

Acknowledgements

Thank you to everyone who helped make this book happen through their edits, revisions, and feedback: Dallas Amsden, Jennifer Bence, Michelle Discavage, Jamie Michel, Dawn Stark, Jenni Ward, and Karen Woolard. Thank you to Bethany Beams for the great cover design.

Thank you to: the girls of RealTalk who dauntlessly live transparently with one another day in and day out; the gang of Dreamers and Builders who help us punch fear in the face; and our cohorts from the Launch Out Intensive who encourage us to launch this dream.

Thank you to Liz Clark, Randy Langley, Mike Loomis, and Ronne Rock for all the hours of brainstorming with us and for asking the right questions.

Special thanks to Dr. Patti Amsden for bringing the Larry Crabb counseling model to our local church and for teaching us to live transparently in community. The revelation of living in a new, redeemed story is based on her teachings. Her feedback for this book was invaluable.